Down by
The Thames

This edition first published in 2012 by
Step Outside Guides.

ISBN 978-1-908921- 01-7
Printed and bound in Great Britain by Berforts Group Ltd.

Acknowledgements
A very special thank you to Sam, who imbued Octavius with such character and fun.

Thank you to all the people who have trialled the trail for us;
Heather, Trinity, Cheyenne, Canaan and Jevae St Lewis
Lorraine, Emily, Jennifer and Bethany Hooper; Claire, Ellie and Lara Hall,
Rowena Howell and Freya Bowker-Howell,
Jen Hale and Phoebe Skinner.

Thanks also to Miranda and Duncan Brown, Joanne Ross and Teresa Solomon for their encouragement, guidance and expertise, and to Emma and Joe Fenn, Charlotte Tizzard and Diane Donat for their editorial input. Many other friends, and our families have helped and contributed in all sorts of ways, and for this we are very grateful.

Front cover pictures from top to bottom:
Oxo Tower, Tower Bridge, Rose Window Winchester Palace
Back cover picture: City Hall

Down by The Thames

For Patricia and Denis Oates

A Step Outside Guide

Contents

Travel Tips

- Travelcards give unrestricted travel on buses, trains and the Underground any time after 9.30am on weekdays, and all day at weekends.

- Tube maps are available free at every Underground station.

- The Transport for London website is *www.tfl.gov.uk*

Introduction

Hello there!

Pleased to meet you.

I'm Octavius Octopus, and I'm going to guide you on today's walk. I live beside the River Thames, and we'll be visiting my home later. I love living in London, and best of all I like dressing up! Look out for me in my different costumes throughout the book.

We're going to walk right through 2,000 years of London's history – all in one day! I've got lots of places and things to show you. Some of them are big and famous, and some are small and hidden, but I've chosen each of them because they are special in some way.

I want you to enjoy my part of London as much as I do, so we're not going to rush along. There are Rest-your-legs pages with fun things to do, and sitting watching London life go by is interesting. As I like to say:
"Let's just see what we can see!"

So look at pages six and seven to check you have everything ready, then we're all set for an amazing day out together.

Here I am, pretending to be a Yeoman Warder at the Tower of London.

How to use your book

Pictures to help you find things

Good picnic spots

 Accessibility information for buggies and wheelchairs

Free toilets

Warning! There are no free toilets until City Hall.
If City Hall is closed, the next free toilets are at Shakespeare's Globe and Tate Modern. There are pay toilets at Tower Hill and behind City Hall.

Top Treasure Alert!

You are about to see one of my special things or places!

 Tick the gold coin when you have seen it.

What to wear or bring with you

 Comfortable shoes

Your picnic

 Pencils and pens for *Rest your legs* pages

Your camera

 Binoculars if you have some

Clothes and extras that suit the weather

IMPORTANT!

- Make sure your group stays together; no-one wants to get lost!
- Don't go inside any of the buildings without an adult.

EYE-SPY lifebelt

On each spread you will see an EYE-SPY lifebelt with a photo of something you can see nearby. Tick the bottom of the belt when you have spotted it.

Buildings information

City Hall

Open Monday - Friday
8.30am - 5.30pm
Closed at weekends
Tel 020 7983 4000
www.london.gov.uk/city-hall

Tate Modern

Open Sunday - Thursday
10.00am - 6.00pm
Friday - Saturday
10.00am - 10.00pm
Tel 020 788 78752
www.tate-org.uk/modern

If you would like to know whether the tide will be high or low, visit
www.tidetimes.org.uk

Accessibility

At the Start

Tower Hill Station does not have lifts to the street: Fenchurch Street and Tower Gateway (DLR) do.

Tower Bridge is accessible by road. On the South bank there is a lift on the Eastern side of the bridge.

At the Finish

There is a lift at each end of Hungerford Bridge West. The East bridge has a lift on the southern side and step free access to Charing Cross Station on the North side.

Roadworks

If there are road works or building repairs there may be a diversion. Just take this as part of London life, and enjoy the detours. You may even discover something wonderful. If you do, then let us know at ***www.stepoutsideguides.com***

READY, STEADY, GO!

Starting Point:
Tower Hill Underground Station
Circle & **District** Lines
(Tower Gateway DLR and Fenchurch St
C2C stations are also very near).

Finishing Point:
Embankment & Charing Cross stations
Circle , **District,** Bakerloo
& **Northern** Lines

Walking distance: About 5km, 3 miles.

Time: About five hours at a leisurely pace, with breaks.

Here we are at Tower Hill Station. Stand at the exit which faces the Tower of London.

We're going up the curving steps ahead of us, for a brilliant introduction to our day. It's also my first Top Treasure.
Can you see what it is?

Waterloo
FINISH
Hungerford
SOUTH

It's a sundial! A very big, very special sundial. (Tick the gold coin.)

The dial shows us a history of London in pictures. It starts when the Romans founded Londinium in 43 AD (or 43 CE) and finishes when the sundial was made, in 2002.

The Sundial
When the sun is shining, the shadow of the **gnomon** (see glossary p32) falls on the circle, and the numbers round the edge tell us the time. If the sun isn't out, it doesn't work!

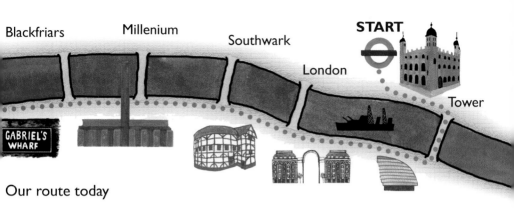

Our route today

Let's take a walk around it and *see what we can see.*

Which is your favourite scene?

....

I like the revolting Peasant's Revolt, and the friendly bus, and Old London Bridge… it's hard to pick just one.

Can you see how many plagues it records?

....

And how how many fires?

....

It's amazing that London is still standing! (Answers p32)

Remember to spy the Eye-Spy!

London has experienced all sorts of **catastrophes** in the last two thousand years. Some are famous, like the Great Plague in 1665, and the Great Fire of London a year later, but the sundial tells us that there were other major plagues and fires too.

London's history is all around us. Look at the Tower of London; the sundial tells us when the first part was built. (Answer on p32)

EYE-SPY

If we look at the Tower there is a stretch of old and crumbly wall on our left. Can you see it? That's Roman. It has been standing there since about 200 AD.
I bet you'd look crumbly too if you'd been standing around for 1,800 years!

As we face The Shard there is a Panoramic Guide. It tells us what all the buildings are. Can you match them up? The Shard isn't shown because it is newer than the guide.

SHARD
On our right is the tallest, and one of the newest buildings in London - the great glass triangle reaching the sky is The Shard, which houses businesses and shops.

Now we go back down the curvy steps, turn right, then right again down more steps. We pass the Roman wall and a statue of the emperor Trajan just beside it, before we go into the subway.

Do you like the bright paintings along the tunnel walls? I think they really cheer it up.

A t the end we can see the Tower of London ahead of us.

We go past the remains of a medieval **postern tower**, and turn right along the path by the **moat**. Information boards here tell us some of the history of the Tower. It looks as though there is loads to read, but don't panic.

The information is in several languages, but only one small part is in English.
Why do you think there are so many languages?

Can you match the phrase 'Well Informed' to its language and its flag?

Well informed		French
Dobro informisani		Japanese
Bene informato		Serbian
歡迎		Norwegian
Bien informe		English
Godt informert		Italian

(Answers p32)

When you've read the information, it's time to move on. Where the path divides, we're going to take the lower path (even though every arrow on the sign board points to the upper path - trust me!)

As we turn the corner, look for arrow slits in the castle walls. The window spaces show how thick the walls are. They were built that way to keep enemies out - and prisoners in!

Look out for Yeomen Warders (sometimes called Beefeaters), in their splendid uniforms.
Are they wearing dark blue or red today?

Pass the hedge steps (don't walk on them!), and the stone steps (you *can* walk on them...).
At the end of the path, we go to the right where there is another info plaque, telling us more of the Tower's story.

As you walk along, watch how the outline of the Tower changes against the sky.

I'm itching to show you the Thames, so let's go through the big black gates ahead, to the river wall. We're going to walk towards Tower Bridge, past Traitors' Gate on our left.

When the moat was filled with water, prisoners were brought here by boat, and taken through Traitors' Gate. Then they were imprisoned, tortured, and often beheaded.

Phew! I'm glad all we're doing is walking past!

How high is the water?
When the tide is high it may be nearly up to the top of the wall; when it is low, you can see the river bed. The difference in height between low and high tide is called the tidal range, and on this part of the River Thames it is round about six metres.

As we walk further along we see more reminders of the Tower's violent history as we pass the cannon, pointing at the river. **Gun salutes** are still given here on special occasions.

INFORMATION For details of when the guns fire salutes, visit: *www.4london.info/londoninformationgunsalutes*

At the end of the Tower, go under the bridge, and then turn sharp right, and look out for Dead Man's Hole on the left.

CROSSING THE RIVER

This is where the bodies of beheaded and drowned people used to be washed up. I hope there are none for us to see today!

Have a nervous peek to check. I'm going to jump in the water now and I'll join you on the other side of the bridge. Here are your crossing instructions.

Octavius's excellent intructions for crossing Tower Bridge

Climb the steps by Dead Man's hole. If you are really lucky, you may see the bridge opening to let a tall boat through. I love it when this happens and the road in front of you goes up into the sky. But usually you'll be able to walk straight on to the bridge. Once you're there, make sure you take a few moments to stand right in the middle, (but on the pavement!) with one foot on each side. You can see the river through the gap. Whenever a bus goes past, it makes your legs feel really funny! Can you imagine how it makes my tentacles tickle? Don't forget to enjoy the view up river into the centre of London.

How old do you think this lovely bridge is? Have a guess. .... (Answer p32)

When you've crossed the river, walk down the steps which you can see in the middle of the bridge pavement. At the bottom of the steps, look to your left, along Butler's Wharf. You'll see a scene that hasn't changed much in over 130 years.

Butler's Wharf

These tall buildings were warehouses which stored goods brought by sea from all over the world.
The iron bridges which are **silhouetted** against the sky were used to move goods between buildings. When the docks closed in the 1970s the buildings became **derelict**. They have now been restored and are used for shops, offices and restaurants.
I think they still look pretty dramatic - do you?

This old postbox is at the bottom of the steps from Tower Bridge. Can you see it?

Hi, I'm back with you, wet and cool and ready to keep you company along the South Bank, where we'll be exploring for the rest of today.
We are going away from Butler's Wharf now, so turn right along the river.

Rest-your-legs page

We can sit on the big steps here at
Potters Field and see what we can see!

Look across the river at the spectacular skyline of the City of London. This changes all the time as old buildings are demolished and new ones are built. There are almost always groups of cranes busy on the latest construction.

Can you see any today?

EYE-SPY

Can you draw a boat going through this picture of Tower Bridge?

A SPIRAL SLOPE

The next building we come to is the tilting City Hall.

This is the home of the Greater London Authority (GLA). We can go inside.

There's a security check, then we go up the spiral walkway.

Along the inside wall of the spiral is my curliest Top Treasure.

It is a poem about London by Ben Okri called 'Lines in Potentis'. It was written in 2002, especially for this building. Read it as you walk up – it has some fantastic lines.

At the top of the public area we may be able to watch the London Assembly at work within their glass-walled chamber. If we're here at the right time, we may even see the Mayor!

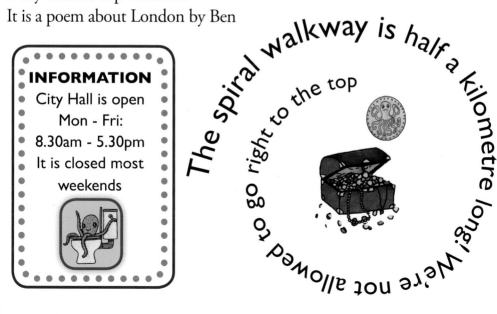

The spiral walkway is half a kilometre long! We're not allowed to go right to the top

The GLA looks after many parts of London life, from policing to public toilets, from transport to the Thames. The Mayor of London is in charge of the GLA - he is not to be confused with the Lord Mayor of London, who is someone completely different!

Back outside City Hall is another Panoramic guide - this one is in three dimensions!

Can you see it? Do you recognise any of the buildings on it?

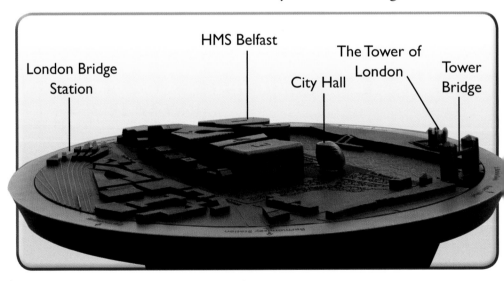

Just past City Hall is a sunken area called The Scoop. There are often free performances to enjoy here in the summer, especially round about lunch-time. You may be lucky and catch one. Keep walking along the riverside to the HMS Belfast.

SHIPS AND SHOPS

The HMS Belfast is a rather scary looking Cruiser. It served the Royal Navy for 32 years from 1939, and now it is a warship museum.

How many guns can you spot as we walk past?
The next special building we come to is Hay's Galleria. This was originally a wharf for unloading tea. When the docks closed the buildings were left to fall apart, but in 1987 they were rescued and restored, and the spectacular glass roof was added. Now the Galleria is an elegant shopping mall.

I tried to help with the anchor once, but I got in a muddle – as you can see!

Eighty per cent of Britain's tea used to arrive here from India, Sri Lanka and China.

Slap bang in the middle of Hay's Galleria is my quirkiest Top Treasure.
It is David Kemp's AMAZING ship sculpture called **The Navigators.**

We can turn down the pathway now, or walk on for a few metres for a photo opportunity.

As water flows through the sculpture, it makes different parts of it move. It changes every minute - and sometimes nothing happens. Let's watch for a few minutes, and see *what we can see.*

Leaving the Galleria, we're going to keep walking along the river until we come to a narrow pathway which is just after some zig-zag railings.

Octavius's Fabulous Photo Idea

 Walk for about one minute to the diagonal granite steps. Going up them makes me feel very peculiar. Does it feel weird with only two legs? Look straight up at the glass buildings and there's your photo! When you've captured those spectacular reflections on your camera, then back to the zig zag railings we go.

EYE-SPY

At the end of the path, we're going to turn right and follow Tooley Street under London Bridge and out the other side.

A PALACE AND A PRISON

When we've passed the lovely Southwark Cathedral, we turn sharp right (see map) to my wettest **Top Treasure** - a full size replica of the Golden Hinde.

We're not going on board, but we will *see what we can see* as we go by.

The Golden Hinde was the first English ship to sail right round the world. It did so in 1577-1580, under the command of Sir Francis Drake.
Can you imagine what it must have been like to be in the middle of a rough ocean in such a tiny ship?

Turn left down Pickfords Wharf, opposite the Golden Hinde and pass the ruins of 12th century Winchester Palace.
Further along the street is the site of a very old prison, The Clink.

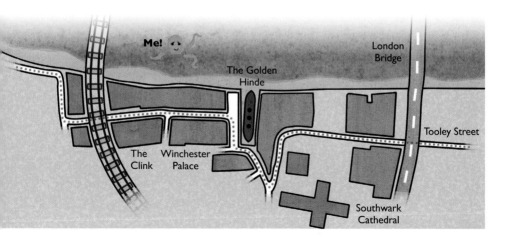

Me!

The Golden Hinde

London Bridge

Tooley Street

The Clink   Winchester Palace

Southwark Cathedral

The Clink was a place of terrible torture, and when rioters burned it down in 1780 it was never rebuilt. But its name lives on as a nickname for all prisons.

London Borough of Southwark
The Clink
1151-1780
Most notorious medieval prison
Voted by the People

What is Terrible torture? Well for example, would you like your feet kept in water until they rotted off? Neither would I!

At the end of the road we turn right, and we're back at the Thames. There's St Paul's Cathedral greeting us from the other side of the river. Isn't it beautiful?
Now we follow the Thames Path under green and gold Southwark Bridge. In the tunnel under the bridge is my coldest Top Treasure; five HUGE pieces of slate carved with rhymes and pictures of Thames Frost Fairs.

In some very harsh winters, the river completely froze over and ice fairs were held actually on the river! There were even bonfires! The slate pictures show us what the fairs were like, and the rhymes tell us what happened, too.

Once we're out of the tunnel-under-the-bridge we're nearly at **MY HOME!**

Detail of Frost Fair slate by David Kindersley

Rest-your-legs page

You could save this page until you are outside the Tate Modern, where there's lots of grass to sit on.

What costumes do you think Octavius would look good in?
You can draw them here!

Do you remember Ben Okri's poem in City Hall, and the old rhyme about the ice fair? Can you make up a rhyme about something we've seen today? Write it in the rope frame.

SHAKESPEARE'S GLOBE

A nd here we are, at Shakespeare's Globe Theatre.

I am proud to live on one of the loveliest things you will see today, and also my Toppiest Top Treasure – the gates to the Globe.

There are 150 sculptures on the gates, and every one is of something in one of Shakespeare's plays.

Which sculpture do you like best?

....

Which ones do other people in your group like?

....

At last you can meet me in the flesh – or rather in the metal!

There are no octopuses in Shakespeare's plays, but on the gate I am dressed as a **Leviathan**. Give me a smile, even though I look a bit scary.

The Leviathan appear in 'A Midsummer Night's Dream'.

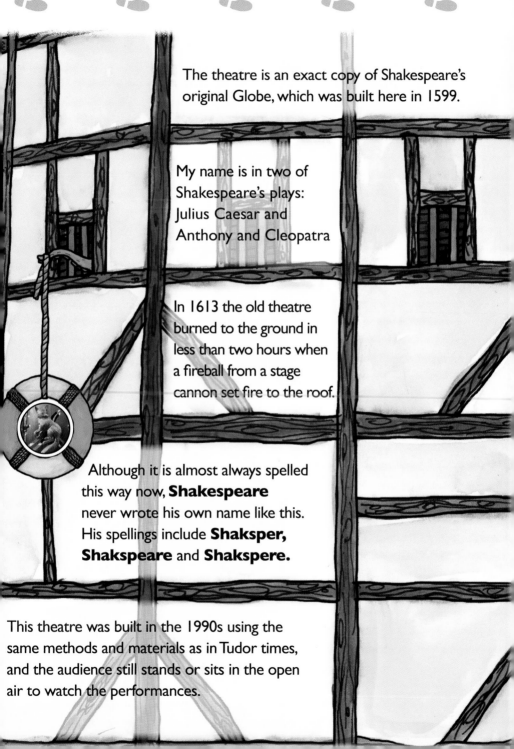

The theatre is an exact copy of Shakespeare's original Globe, which was built here in 1599.

My name is in two of Shakespeare's plays: Julius Caesar and Anthony and Cleopatra

In 1613 the old theatre burned to the ground in less than two hours when a fireball from a stage cannon set fire to the roof.

Although it is almost always spelled this way now, **Shakespeare** never wrote his own name like this. His spellings include **Shaksper, Shakspeare** and **Shakspere.**

This theatre was built in the 1990s using the same methods and materials as in Tudor times, and the audience still stands or sits in the open air to watch the performances.

TATE MODERN

Let's walk on, past a couple of beautiful old houses.

And here we are at the absolutely ENORMOUS Tate Modern Art Gallery. I hang out here occasionally myself and paint; you should see how fast I can finish a picture!

Tate Modern

This building was a working power station until 1981. After that it was left empty until 2000, when this amazing gallery opened. Do have a wander and *see what you can see*. The windows upstairs look out over the river, and even have seats!

Entrance: free
Opening hours: Daily 10.00am – 6.00pm,
Friday & Saturday 10.00am – 10.00pm

This is the largest brick building in Europe.

How many bricks do you think there are?

(Answer on p32)

EYE-SPY

Here is the grass I promised you on page 23 to rest-your-legs. When you are rested and revived, there are more wonderful sights and Top Treasures in store, so let's go! The next bridge we come to is Blackfriars. In the tunnel under the bridge are very large copies of engravings which show how the old bridge was built.

INFORMATION
If you have run out of time, you can walk over the Millennium Bridge, just by the Tate, to St. Paul's station on the Central Line.

Blackfriars Bridge marks the 'tidal turning point' of the Thames. It is reckoned to have salt water downstream from here, and fresh water upstream. So on the downstream side of the bridge pillars, (which we come to first), there are carvings of seabirds, and on the other side there are carvings of freshwater birds. Can you spot them?

A TASTY TOWER

The Oxo Tower Story

In the 1920s, the warehouses (which are now shops) were built by the makers of OXO, and they wanted to put advertisements on the tower. This wasn't allowed, but the architect designed the tower so that each side has three windows; a circle, a cross and another circle. This just happens to make the word OXO! At night, with lights on inside the tower, they glow out much more brightly than any advert! And they've lasted much longer too. Cheeky, but clever!

O n we go, towards my biggest Top Treasure.

Past the grand Sea Containers House is a long, red brick building called Oxo Tower Wharf. Walk out on to the pier just here, and look back at the building. Can you see the word OXO up each side of the tower? That's my Top Treasure!

Do you remember back by Tower Bridge, I said that the river has high and low tides? Well, just here by the Oxo Tower Wharf people sometimes go down onto the river beach at low tide and look for interesting objects. I sneak down there a lot. Sometimes people find pieces of old pottery, Tudor hair pins or even Roman coins.

If you go down to the beach, make sure that it is safe, and that the adults in your party are happy to go with you.

EYE-SPY

On we go and soon we come to **Gabriel's Wharf,** another historic dock that is now used for shops and restaurants.
As we walk in, it looks as though there is a row of tall houses on the right. But look closely, and you will see that they are all just painted on a plain brick wall!
Just by Gabriel's Wharf is my sandiest **Top Treasure**; it is a beach, which you can see at low tide.

Sand sculptors create all sorts of objects and scenes here. When the tide comes in again the sculptures will all be washed away, but meanwhile, you are invited to throw coins down.

SOUTH BANK

Soon we come to the South Bank Centre. It is the largest arts centre in the world!

Walk under Waterloo Bridge and past the book market. Underneath one of the concert halls is my last and most colourful **Top Treasure.**

It is a space covered in graffiti and it doesn't look very treasurish. However there are often skateboarders and stunt bikers here, and they are great fun to watch. I can perform some amazing stunts on my bike! When we've passed the Festival Hall, we have reached Hungerford Bridge where we cross the river.

There are steps or a lift onto the bridge. Buskers often play here. Some are very good indeed – and some are not!

I like to have a play myself now and then – I make a terrific One Man Band!

This is one of my favourite views of London. Can you see the OXO Tower? How many other sights from our day can you spot?

At the end of the bridge, continue straight on to Charing Cross station or turn right down the steps to Embankment tube station. Here I must leave you. I hope you've enjoyed our day as much as I have! I'm going to jump back in the water now and swim back home to the Globe Theatre.

Bye bye, and as Mr Shakespeare might say -

fare thee well!

GLOSSARY & ANSWERS

GLOSSARY

p8 Gnomon – the part of a sundial that casts the shadow. It is a Greek word, meaning 'indicator'.

p9 Catastrophe – a large scale, horrible event.

p11 Postern Tower – a tower guarding a rear or side entrance to a castle.

p11 Moat – a pool of water around the castle to protect it. The Tower's moat is dry now, and grassed over.

p13 Gun Salute – a number of guns fire blank shots, one after the other.

p15 Silhouette – The outline shape of an object. Here I've used it to describe the shape a building makes against the sky.

p15 Derelict – Falling apart because it isn't used any more.

p20 Navigator – The person on board ship who works out and records exactly where the ship is.

p24 Leviathan – Sea monster.

p27 Pillar – A vertical support. Pillars hold up the road or railway route across the river.

ANSWERS

p9: There were four plagues and three major fires. **p10**: The Tower of London was founded in 1066 and building started in the 1070s.

P11: Flag puzzle:

	Serbia - Dobro informisani
	Italy - Bene informato
	United Kingdom - Well informed
	France - Bien informe
	Norway - Godt informert
	Japan - 歓迎

P15: Tower Bridge is not as old as it looks; it was built in 1895. **P26**: The Tate Modern has about 4,200,000 bricks.

EYE - SPY

p9 Skeleton from Sundial

p10 Emperor Trajan

p13 Arrow slit from Tower

p15 Top of Tower Bridge

p16 Tower of London **p18** The Gherkin

p20 A Navigator **p23** St Paul's Cathedral

p25 Fox from globe gate **p27** Detail from Blackfriar's Bridge **p29** Riverside lamp

p31 Wind Turbine South Bank Centre